FREEDOM AT A COST

by
Jeremy F. Bender

authorHOUSE®

AuthorHouse™
1663 Liberty Drive, Suite 200
Bloomington, IN 47403
www.authorhouse.com
Phone: 1-800-839-8640

First published by AuthorHouse 11/05/07

ISBN: 978-1-4259-9035-0 (sc)

Library of Congress Control Number: 2007907796

Printed in the United States of America
Bloomington, Indiana

This book is printed on acid-free paper.

Freedom at a Cost is dedicated to:
My Father

Freedom at a Cost from the Author

Written By Jeremy Bender, "FREEDOM AT
A COST" is my creative presentation of social
commentary constructed entirely from beginning each
statement with the word F-R-E-E-D-O-M, among the
issues I touch upon are war, poverty, America's image
in the world, the environment and education. The
messages consistently stress my views in a passionate
manner. It will provoke thought and discussion, while
raising awareness to the motives behind much of
society's individual actions, and as a whole around
the World. In today's uncertain times, it may be
regarded as topical and relevant by many.

Freedom at a Cost

Work Prepared By Jeremy F. Bender

FIRST

REALIZE

EVERYONE

EVENTUALLY

DIES

OFTEN

MISLOOKED

FREEDOM

RIGHTS

EQUALITY

EVERYTHING

DEPENDS

ON

MONEY

FOREIGN

RELATIONS

ERODE

EVERYDAY

DESTROYING

OUR

MIGHT

FACE

REALITY

ENTER

EACH

DAY

OPEN

MINDED

FRIENDS

RELATIVES

EVERYONE

ELSE

DEPRESSED

OVER

MEMORIES

FIRST
RESPONSE
EMERGENCY
EMPLOYEES
DIED
OVER
MONEY

FRUSTRATION

RESENTMENT

ENCOMPASSES

EVERYBODY

DISHEARTENING

OUR

MILITARY

FIND
REMEDIES
ERASE
EMOTIONS
DIVIDE
OUR
MONEY

FOR
RELIGIONS TO
EXIST
EVERYBODY
DEVELOPS
OWN
MIND-SET

FIND
REASONS
ENDURE
EDUCATION
DECIDE
OTHERWISE
MISS OUT

FLAGS
RAISED
EVERYDAY
EVERYBODY
DISPLAYING
OUR
MANHUNTS

FOREIGNERS

RELOCATE

EVERYDAY

EACH

DRIVEN BY

OPPORTUNITY

MONEY

FAITHLESS
REIGN
ENABLES
ELUSIVE
DIPLOMACY
OCCASIONAL
MISCONDUCT

FASCISM

RACISM

ETHICAL

ERADICATION

DEFINITELY

OPPRESSES

MAN

FOR

RIGHTEOUS

EXISTENCE

EDUCATION

DAILY

ORIGINATES

MATURITY

FANTASY
REALITY
EARTHQUAKES
EROSION
DESTROYING
OUTER SPACE
MOTHER-EARTH

FREEDOM
RIDICULOUS
EARN
EACH
DOLLAR
ON
MINIMUM—WAGE

FIGHTING

RESUMES

EACH AND

EVERY

DAY

OVER

MONEY

FALSE
REPORTS
EACH
EXAMPLES OF
DISTURBINGLY
OBVIOUS
MALICE

FAILURE
RECTIFYING
EMOTIONS
EVENTUALLY
DESTROYS
ONES
MIND

FATIGUE

RESISTANCE

EXHAUSTION

EXAMPLES

DAILY

OPERATIONS OF OUR

MILITARY

FRIGHTENED
RESERVES
ENGAGED IN
EMERGENCY
DEFENSIVE
OFFENSIVE
MODES

FAILING TO
RECOGNIZE
EACH AND
EVERY
DEATH
OFFENDS
MOTHERS

FATHERS

REGRET

EVER

ENLISTING

DELIBERATELY INTO

OUR

MILITARY

FIGHTING'S
RIGHT
EVERYONE
ENLIST
DEPLOY
OUR
MILITARY

FIGHTING'S

RIDICULOUS

EVERYONE

ELSE

DESPISES

OUR

MILITARY

FRAIL

REMAINS

EVENTUALLY

EMERGE

DEPENDING

ON

MIND-POWER

FORCED
RETALIATION
EMPOWERS
ENABLES
DESTRUCTION
OF
MASSES

FORTUNES
RANSACKED
ENTIRE
EMPIRES
DESTROYED
OVER
MONEY

FINANCIAL

RECORDS

EXPLODING

ENRON

DISCOVERY

ONLY

MINOR

FACES
REARRANGED
EYES
EARS
DISFIGUREMENT
OPTIONAL
MEMORIES

FIXED

RACES

EVERY

ELECTION

DEPENDS

ON

MONEY

FUNCTIONALITY
RETURNS
EVENTUALLY
ENDING
DAYS
OF
MISERY

FALSIFIED
REPORTS
EDITED
EXPLANATION
DOCUMENTS
OVERLOOKING
MISCONDUCTS

FIGHT

RETALIATE

ENGAGE

EMBATTLE

DESTROY

OVERPOWER

MASSACRE

FEAR

REPLACES

EVERYONE

ELSE'S

DOUBT

OF

MISCONDUCT

FAILURE

RELOCATING

EMOTIONS

ENEMIES

DESTROYING

OUR

MINDS

FORCED
RELOCATIONS
ENEMIES
ENRAGED
DESTROYING
OUR
MILITARY

FORCED

RESTRUCTURING

EVERY TIME

EACH

DICTATOR

OVERTHROWS

MASSES

FRANTIC

RELATIVES

ENDURING

ENDLESS

DAYS

OF

MISERY

FORGET

REPLACING

EVERYTHING

ENTIRE

DREAMS

ONLY

MEMORIES

FEED

REPLENISH

EDUCATE

ENLIGHTEN

DISCOVER

ORGANIZE

MATURE

FORMULAS

REMEDIES

ELIXIRS

EVERYONE

DRUGGED

OR

MEDICATED

FOREST−FIRES

RAINFORESTS

EROSION

EARTHQUAKES

DEPLETION

OZONE

MISS USE

FREEWAYS
ROADS
EVERYWHERE
EVERYONE
DRIVING
OVER
MOTHER EARTH

FUNERALS
REMIND
EVERYONE
EACH
DAY
ONLY
MINISCULE

FORECLOSURE

RELOCATION

EVICTION

ENDLESS

DEVELOPMENT

OWED

MONTHLY

FURTHER

RAMIFICATIONS

ERODING

EARTH WILL BE THE

DESTRUCTION

OF

MANKIND

FITNESS

RECREATION

EXERCISE

EATING

DETERMINES

OBESITY OF

MAN

FLOODS

RAVISHING

EARTH

ERODING

DREAMS

OF

MANY

FASCINATING
REALITY
EVERYTHING
EDUCATION
DOES
OFTEN
MATTERS

FREEDOM
REMAINS
EVERYONE'S
ENDLESS
DREAMS
OF
MONEY

FOCUS THE
REMAINDER OF THE
EARTHS
EXISTENCE
DEPENDS
ON
MAN

FACT

REMAINS

EVERYONE'S

EVENTUALLY

DESTROYED

OVER

MONEY

FUTURISTIC

RESEARCH

ENTERTAINS

EVERYONE

DEPENDENT ONLY

ON

MACHINES

FOREIGN

REGIONS

EXECUTE

EACH OTHER

DAILY

OVER

MONEY

FIND

REMEDIES

EVEN–OUT

EVERYONE'S

DISBURSEMENT

OF

MONEY

FAMILIES
RARELY
EXERCISE
EVENTUALLY
DEVELOPING
OBESITY AND
MASSIVENESS

FAIR
REASONABLE
EQUAL
EQUALITY
DIVIDED
OVER
MONEY

FRIENDS

REMAIN

EQUALS

EXTREMELY

DEPENDABLE

OPINIONS

MATTER

Failure
Remaining
Educated
Eventually
Deteriorates
Ones
Mind

FORENSIC

RESEARCH

EVENTUALLY

ENDS

DEPRESSION

OF

MOTHERS

FATHERLESS

REBELS

EXPLODING

EXPLOSIONS

DESTROYING

OUR

MILITARY

FREQUENCIES
RADIOS
EVERYBODY'S
ELECTRONIC
DEVICES
OFTEN
MONITORED

FACING
RELENTLESS
EMOTIONAL
ENGAGEMENTS
DEFENDING
OPERATION
MANIPULATOR

FAILURE

RELEASING

EVIDENCE

ENTERTAINS

DECEPTION

OF

MAN

FORTUNATELY

REASONABLY

EDUCATED

EARS

DECIPHER

ON–GOING

MISCUES

FRANTICALLY

RACING

ERASE

EVERY

DOCUMENT

OR

MISTAKE

FREAKS
RETARDS
ECCENTRIC
EMOTIONALLY
DISABLED
ONLY
MIRACLES

FREEDOM

REQUIRES

ELIMINATING

EXECUTING

DESTROYING

ORDERING

MURDERS

FINALLY

REMEMBER

ENTER

EACH

DAY

OPEN

MINDED